The secret history of a private man. By Francis Wollaston, ...

Francis Wollaston

ECCO
PRINT EDITIONS

Eighteenth Century
Collections Online
Print Editions

Gale ECCO Print Editions

Relive history with *Eighteenth Century Collections Online*, now available in print for the independent historian and collector. This series includes the most significant English-language and foreign-language works printed in Great Britain during the eighteenth century, and is organized in seven different subject areas including literature and language; medicine, science, and technology; and religion and philosophy. The collection also includes thousands of important works from the Americas.

The eighteenth century has been called "The Age of Enlightenment." It was a period of rapid advance in print culture and publishing, in world exploration, and in the rapid growth of science and technology – all of which had a profound impact on the political and cultural landscape. At the end of the century the American Revolution, French Revolution and Industrial Revolution, perhaps three of the most significant events in modern history, set in motion developments that eventually dominated world political, economic, and social life.

In a groundbreaking effort, Gale initiated a revolution of its own: digitization of epic proportions to preserve these invaluable works in the largest online archive of its kind. Contributions from major world libraries constitute over 175,000 original printed works. Scanned images of the actual pages, rather than transcriptions, recreate the works *as they first appeared.*

Now for the first time, these high-quality digital scans of original works are available via print-on-demand, making them readily accessible to libraries, students, independent scholars, and readers of all ages.

For our initial release we have created seven robust collections to form one the world's most comprehensive catalogs of 18th century works.

Initial Gale ECCO Print Editions collections include:

History and Geography

Rich in titles on English life and social history, this collection spans the world as it was known to eighteenth-century historians and explorers. Titles include a wealth of travel accounts and diaries, histories of nations from throughout the world, and maps and charts of a world that was still being discovered. Students of the War of American Independence will find fascinating accounts from the British side of conflict.

Social Science
Delve into what it was like to live during the eighteenth century by reading the first-hand accounts of everyday people, including city dwellers and farmers, businessmen and bankers, artisans and merchants, artists and their patrons, politicians and their constituents. Original texts make the American, French, and Industrial revolutions vividly contemporary.

Medicine, Science and Technology
Medical theory and practice of the 1700s developed rapidly, as is evidenced by the extensive collection, which includes descriptions of diseases, their conditions, and treatments. Books on science and technology, agriculture, military technology, natural philosophy, even cookbooks, are all contained here.

Literature and Language
Western literary study flows out of eighteenth-century works by Alexander Pope, Daniel Defoe, Henry Fielding, Frances Burney, Denis Diderot, Johann Gottfried Herder, Johann Wolfgang von Goethe, and others. Experience the birth of the modern novel, or compare the development of language using dictionaries and grammar discourses.

Religion and Philosophy
The Age of Enlightenment profoundly enriched religious and philosophical understanding and continues to influence present-day thinking. Works collected here include masterpieces by David Hume, Immanuel Kant, and Jean-Jacques Rousseau, as well as religious sermons and moral debates on the issues of the day, such as the slave trade. The Age of Reason saw conflict between Protestantism and Catholicism transformed into one between faith and logic -- a debate that continues in the twenty-first century.

Law and Reference
This collection reveals the history of English common law and Empire law in a vastly changing world of British expansion. Dominating the legal field is the *Commentaries of the Law of England* by Sir William Blackstone, which first appeared in 1765. Reference works such as almanacs and catalogues continue to educate us by revealing the day-to-day workings of society.

Fine Arts
The eighteenth-century fascination with Greek and Roman antiquity followed the systematic excavation of the ruins at Pompeii and Herculaneum in southern Italy; and after 1750 a neoclassical style dominated all artistic fields. The titles here trace developments in mostly English-language works on painting, sculpture, architecture, music, theater, and other disciplines. Instructional works on musical instruments, catalogs of art objects, comic operas, and more are also included.

The BiblioLife Network

This project was made possible in part by the BiblioLife Network (BLN), a project aimed at addressing some of the huge challenges facing book preservationists around the world. The BLN includes libraries, library networks, archives, subject matter experts, online communities and library service providers. We believe every book ever published should be available as a high-quality print reproduction; printed on-demand anywhere in the world. This insures the ongoing accessibility of the content and helps generate sustainable revenue for the libraries and organizations that work to preserve these important materials.

The following book is in the "public domain" and represents an authentic reproduction of the text as printed by the original publisher. While we have attempted to accurately maintain the integrity of the original work, there are sometimes problems with the original work or the micro-film from which the books were digitized. This can result in minor errors in reproduction. Possible imperfections include missing and blurred pages, poor pictures, markings and other reproduction issues beyond our control. Because this work is culturally important, we have made it available as part of our commitment to protecting, preserving, and promoting the world's literature.

GUIDE TO FOLD-OUTS MAPS and OVERSIZED IMAGES

The book you are reading was digitized from microfilm captured over the past thirty to forty years. Years after the creation of the original microfilm, the book was converted to digital files and made available in an online database.

In an online database, page images do not need to conform to the size restrictions found in a printed book. When converting these images back into a printed bound book, the page sizes are standardized in ways that maintain the detail of the original. For large images, such as fold-out maps, the original page image is split into two or more pages

Guidelines used to determine how to split the page image follows:

• Some images are split vertically; large images require vertical and horizontal splits.
• For horizontal splits, the content is split left to right.
• For vertical splits, the content is split from top to bottom.
• For both vertical and horizontal splits, the image is processed from top left to bottom right.

from the Dict

4 9 0 2 d d 1

Bps Ely's Sale
Nov 1808

To Mr Forster,
from C.I. Inglis
Oct 10. 1808.

4902. dd. 1.

This Book, intituled,
The Secret History of a Private Man,
by Francis Wollaston; L.L.B. F.R.S.
is extremely scarce.

It was never published; a few Copies
only were printed; and given by
Mr. Wollaston to his particular Friends.
It appears by a Manuscript on the other
side of this Leaf, that this Book was
the Property of the late Hon.ble Dr.
Yorke Bishop of Ely; to whom in all
Probability it was presented by Mr.
Wollaston, as the Hon.ble Dr. Yorke and
Mr. Wollaston were very intimate.
At the Sale of the Hon.ble Dr. Yorke's
Library in Nov.r 1808 it seems by the
same Manuscript to have been purchased
by a Mr. Inglis, and given by him to
the late Rev.d Dr. Gosset. At the Sale
of the Rev.d Dr. Gosset's Library by Leigh & Sotheby on
June 7. 1813 and 22 following Days
it was purchased by me.
R. D. Shackleford

SECRET HISTORY

OF A

PRIVATE MAN.

BY

FRANCIS WOLLASTON,
LL.B. F.R.S.

Ὁ Σωκράτης· Εἰπέ μοι, ἔφη ὦ Ἐυθύδημε, εἰς Δελφὰς ἤδη πώποτε ἀφίκε, Καὶ δὶς, νὴ Δἰ', ἔφη. Κατέμαθες ἂν πρὸς τῷ ναῷ πε γεγραμμένον τὸ, Γνῶθι σαυτόν, Ἔγωγε Πότερον ἒν, ἒδέν σοι τε γράμματος εμέλησεν, ἢ προσέσχες τὲ καὶ ἐπεχείρησας σαυτὸν ἐπισκοπεῖν ὅτις ἔιης,

Xenophon Ed Leuncl p 796

Ἐν τέτῳ γνώσονται πάντες ὅτι ἐμοὶ μαθηταί εςε, ἐὰν ἀγάπην ἔχητε ἐν ἀλλήλοις.

Joan. XIII 35

𝔏𝔬𝔫𝔡𝔬𝔫:

PRINTED IN THE YEAR M.DCC.XCV.

Every Man is important to himfelf. It is
wifely ordained by the Great Author of our
Nature, that we fhould be fo, in fome degree;
in order to move us to action, and render us
beneficial to each other: though moft of us
are but too apt to flatter ourfelves, that we are
of greater importance to the world, than the
generality will allow.

It is very poffible that may be the cafe with
refpect to the Author of the following pages;
who, though he has paffed his life in a private
ftation, has determined to fet down upon
paper fome leading occurrences of it, to-
gether with the real motives by which he has
been actuated: thinking that fuch a detail, if
it does no other good, may at leaft afford fome
ufeful leffons, to thofe who fhall choofe to read
what they will find here written.

One

One thing the Reader, whoever he be, fhould underftand; that inftances of bright parts, or fhining abilities, muft not be looked-for in one, who never pretended to them. An honeft heart, and a good intention throughout life, he feels confcious he may claim, as well as fincerity in this declaration of his views. He knows that he is not without his errors; fome of which he may point out, while others may be difcerned which efcape him. But, having been accuftomed from early life to examine himfelf, and to think much, he has never been afhamed to acknowledge a miftake, when it has been made known to him. To perfift in one, he has always efteemed a greater blot on any character.

To trace a long line of anceftors, as he has been told the Heralds' Office can fhew in his family for two or three centuries, is of little concern to onefelf, and of none to others. It is well known, that we all derive our pedigree originally from Adam. If we have had the happinefs of being born of reputable Parents; who, from being in eafy circumftances had the power, and who had the heart to beftow

on

on us a good education; for that we have reafon to be thankful. It reflects no merit upon us. But it is a call upon us, to make a proper ufe of the advantage which that gives us, in ftepping forth into the world.

FRANCIS WOLLASTON, the fubject of thefe papers, was born November 23, 1731 old ftyle. He was the eldeft fon of Francis Wollafton, of Charterhoufe-fquare efquire; who was third fon of William Wollafton, Clerc, of the fame place: the Author of, *the Religion of Nature delineated*; whofe character is well known. The Father received a private education at home under the Grandfather, as the fon did under the Father. and poffibly to that caufe may be afcribed, the thoughtful turn which was impreffed fo early upon the mind For, though he acknowledges himfelf indebted to thofe who were fet over him as Tutors in the languages, and particularly to Dr. Robert Glynn of King's College Cambridge, whofe kind attention towards him was continued after he went to the univerfity, and during the whole

of

of his abode there, the particular bias towards religion, and philosophy, and scientific pursuits, he feels to have imbibed from his Father, whose memory he must ever revere.

From home he went in June 1748, with his next brother Charlton, to Sidney College Cambridge, where many of his family, and two of his sons, have received their education, and to which he trusts they have done no discredit

His original destination was to the Study of the Law. And he was accordingly admitted at Lincoln's Inn, November 1750; and began to direct his thoughts that way. But he soon discerned, that it was a Profession ill suited to his disposition. The labour of that study he did not fear Neither did he despair of being able, in some degree, to qualify himself for the Bar. But the idea of being to hold himself ready, to defend either side of any question, as clients should happen to retain him, he could not digest. This struck him, long before he mentioned it to any one. And this turned his mind towards the Church; in which he thought himself sure, of never

being

being to defend a pofition, which he did not fully in his heart, and from conviction, judge to be the truth.

Yet, in a matter of fuch importance, he determined not to be too hafty. It was to govern his life The Clerical Office he confidered as one, not to be taken up without mature reflection: and therefore, while he was profecuting his academical ftudies, and fuch as might be preparatory to either of the two Profeffions, even after he thought he had fettled his determination, he refolved to allow himfelf yet a full year more, for difpaffionate confideration, and an examination of himfelf.

During that interval, he took all opportunities of confulting fuch books as appeared to him beft to try his heart, and to inform his judgement, particularly Bifhop Burnet's Paftoral Care, and ferioufly weighing every part of it. And, at the expiration of the term which he had prefcribed to himfelf, having then fully made up his mind upon the fubject, that it was a Profeffion he could like to undertake, and one in which he thought

he

he could become more useful in the world than in any other way; he wrote to his Father from College, fully to explain himself And, on receiving his answer, he went immediately to London, to converse with him and consult him upon it.

To the Father it was very far from defagreeable: especially in the way the son had been led to the determination. It was thereupon agreed, that he should return to College and, having then passed the time of keeping exercise for the degree of bachelor in Arts, that he should proceed in Law.

In relation to his studies in Divinity, he owes it to the memory of an old Friend of his Father, to confess, that he received more information concerning them from him, though a Layman, than from any of the Clergy who ever came in his way. He means Daniel Wray esq. late a Deputy-Teller in his Majesty's Exchequer, under the second Earl of Hardwicke: a Gentleman of great vivacity and bright parts, with a most uncommon degree of learning, and knowledge in various branches of literature, and one

of

of the beft Friends that a Young Man could have as an acquaintance. He had long been intimate in the Lord Chancellor Hardwicke's family: and had been affiftant with his advice to all the younger branches of it. So he was to the Author of thefe pages, and to his Brothers· and he continued the fame kindnefs, as long as his life was prolonged, to the Author's fons as they began to grow up. Courting the acquaintance of young men, and ftudying to make his houfe and his company agreeable to them, he was always open to be afked advice; and never backward of giving it freely in a moft kind way unafked, where he faw occafion.

This is faid, not in the fpirit of flattery towards one who is far out of the reach of flattery, but as a hint to thofe who may read thefe pages, to do the fame as far as their abilities extend: and to young men to feek out, and to cultivate the acquaintance of fuch perfons, wherever they can find them.

Not having any particular Preferment in view; nor any neceffity to undertake a Curacy

from

from pecuniary confiderations, Mr. W. took
Deacon's Orders at the regular time fpecified
by the rubric, at the general ordination next
after he was twenty-three, and thofe of Prieft
when he was twenty-four years of age compleat, returning to College, and refiding there
a year longer than he would otherwife have
chofen to do it; that he might introduce two
more of his Brothers, who came thither at
that time, into proper company; and affift
them with his advice Indeed, from the time
he began to be of any ftanding in the Univerfity, he thought he found it of great fervice to young men, at their firft coming, to
be led into a right path, and thereupon he
had always endeavored, as far as it was in
his power, to do that office for thofe who
fell in his way. Such near relations had a
right to claim it.

At the latter end of 1756 he took his leave
of a college life, and returned to his father's
houfe· and about Chriftmas in that year, he
undertook the Sunday morning preaching at
St Ann's Soho, for Dr. Squire, afterwards
Bifhop of St. David's; who had juft at that
time

time been appointed Clerc of the closet to his present Majesty then prince of Wales; and who had asked Mr. Wray to recommend to him an assistant, to supply his place in that pulpit. Mr. Wray immediately thought of Mr. Wollaston; and strongly advised him, not to decline it: For, though he allowed that it was an arduous task to begin at once to preach before such a congregation, among whom at that time were three Bishops, he obligingly added, that it need not be feared; and would be such an initiation, as would constrain a young man to exert himself, and render every thing afterward easy.

In that station he continued till the beginning of the summer 1758: When he married Miss Althea Hyde, fifth daughter of John Hyde esq of Charterhouse Square. And, out of delicacy, he declined officiating any longer at St. Ann's; lest it should hurt the feelings of a young Lady of that parish, with whom a connection had been proposed two years before.

In the course of that summer, he was instituted to the Rectory of Dengey in Essex,

on

on the prefentation of Simon Fanfhawe efq. But, there being no houfe upon it, nor any one which could be hired, he continued in one he had taken at Richmond in Surrey, near to his Father's fummer refidence, till after the living of Eaft Dereham in Norfolk became vacant, of which his Father had a few years before obtained the Advowfon.

As foon as the Vicarage-houfe could be ready, (which indeed was not till the fpring of 1763, as he was obliged to rebuild the greateft part of it) he removed to Eaft Dereham; and continued there, only occafionally vifiting his Parents, till 1769, when, by the favour of Dr Zachary Pearce, Bifhop of Rochefter, he was collated to the Rectory of Chiflehurft in Kent; which has ever fince been his principal Refidence. On that occafion the Vicarage of Eaft Dereham was ceded of courfe, though the Rectory, being an appropriate Sinecure, was retained

At Chiflehurft he felt himfelf comfortable: having a Parifh entirely to his mind; and within a few miles of his Father and Mother, who

who were growing infirm, and then fettled folely in Charterhoufe Square.

Yet he had not been there two years, before a matter was agitated, which much engaged his thoughts. And the part which he took in it, having been greatly mifunderftood, or fadly mifreprefented, it has appeared to him to deferve to be ftated fairly by one who muft know beft his own defigns; that thofe who come after him, or any who choofe to concern themfelves about it, may underftand the whole of what really was done.

When he entered on the ftudy of Divinity, it never was his intention *jurare in verba magiftri*; but to embrace Truth wherever he could find it, and to follow whitherfoever it fhould lead him. Before he took his degree, he read'd over the Articles he was to fign; and not only the articles, but the Books of Homilies: and he felt fo well fatisfied with Bifhop Burnet's Expofition of the former, and the good intention of the latter, that he confcientioufly could fet his Name to them. For fome time after he was in Orders, he was ftrictly what people affect to call Orthodox, almoft almoſt according to the higheſt acceptation of that term   Yet he *then* could, and *he* then did feel for others who were not ſo *orthodox* as himſelf and he therefore did not even then read the Athanaſian Creed before any congregation : though, after mentioning his reaſons for omitting it, he has always left it to his Curates to uſe their own diſcretion when they officiated in his ſtead.   He was told, from high authority, that, to uſe the words of a great Prelate, " it is to be wiſhed that we were well " rid of it " but he was aſſured, that if a Clergyman thought it beſt to neglect reading it , the omiſſion which could not be authorized, might be connived at.   For his part, whatever be the Doctrines of that Creed (founded as they appear therein to be, on an ænigmatic confuſion of ideas, and of language) the Damnatory Clauſes, he always thought highly unfit to come from the mouth of a true diſciple of Chriſt.

As he proſecuted his Studies at Dereham, he began to waver on ſome points of the received doctrine, which he had thought clear But he again reconciled himſelf to

the

the explanations given of them. Perhaps he was, more than he ought, inclined fo to do. For, having engaged in the Ministry, and thinking that he was doing good in it, he certainly was unwilling to let any unnecessary fcruples turn him afide, and render him incapable of continuing useful in that line

After he got to Chiflehurft, Questions of that nature began to be debated openly. A Society affembled at the Feathers Tavern, drew up a Petition which they prefented to the Houfe of Commons, for the entire abolition of Subfcription to any Articles of Faith whatfoever. Though refufed to be received by the majority in that Houfe, February 6, 1772, yet the Debate upon it, gave rife to a great deal of talk among all ranks of men; but more efpecially among the Clergy, and the Members of the two Univerfities Mr. W, knowing his fentiments, which till that time he had kept within his own breaft, thought it his Duty then to explain himfelf to thofe to whom he held himfelf amenable; and waited on the Archbifhop, and the Bifhop of his Diocefe, to declare his difapprobation

probation of the eftablifhed mode of fubfcription, and his wifh to fee that amended, but
expreffing at the fame time, his difapprobation too, of the length to which the late
Petition had extended, in which he therefore had not joined, and of the manner in
which redrefs had been defired in an eccle-
fiaftical matter, without confulting their ec-
clefiaftical fuperiors upon it.

In the beginning of the following Summer, he was appointed to preach the Vifita-
tion Sermon at Bromley in Kent, before Mr.
Archdeacon Law and he confidered that, as
a fort of call upon him to declare his fentiments yet more openly. He did fo But,
though invited by fome of the Clergy prefent,
to make that difcourfe public; he, who never
would diffemble his opinions, never was de-
firous of obtruding them upon others; and
faw no advantage that could accrue to the
public, from his appearing in print.

But before the clofe of the year, he was
induced to think differently on that head.
For, learning that the Petition to Parliament
from the Feathers Tavern, was intended to be
renewed

renewed the enfuing Seffion, and finding in the mean time, that very many of the Clergy, who were like himfelf unwilling to join with the Petitioners, wifhed to fee the affair of Subfcription taken up by the Bifhops them-felves, and reduced to fome lefs exception-able terms, it occurred to him, and he was therein fupported by the advice of feveral very refpectable friends, that it might be of feafonable fervice to the public, to fet on foot fome application from the Clergy to the Bench of Bifhops, to defire them to undertake it. This thought gave rife to his *Addrefs to the Clergy*; which he publifhed in November 1772; fending a copy to each of the Bifhops, and difperfing them to every part of the king-dom.

One of the Bench, when he waited upon him with it; and to whom he was making an apology for not having confulted him before the publication, replied, " You did right, not " to fhew it to any of us. It is then res in-" tegra to us all." " I hope," added he, " You do not infinuate that we are againft " an alteration in the forms of fubfcription;

4   " for

" for I affure you we are moft of us for it:
" all indeed excepting three or four, but they
" are great ones" Whom he meaned, he
did not explain, and it did not become the
Author to afk. Yet he thought he knew
afterwards

The Archbifhop (Cornwallis, than whom
there never was a more benevolent or lefs
affuming Prelate) who had faid that " fome-
" thing muft be done", feemed much to approve of the fcheme. And it was through
his advice, that a fecond very large edition
was printed, becaufe he wifhed that the Addrefs to the Clergy might be circulated yet
more fully.

Bifhop Pearce was as liberal in his fentiments concerning fubfcriptions, as any of
his Brethren But he had conceived an idea,
that the Act of Union with Scotland, had
precluded all alterations. And he never
could be convinced of the contrary; though
the Church of Scotland had itfelf altered its
Formula of Subfcription, after that union.

Many others on the bench of Bifhops,
were pleafed to declare their approbation.

From

From the Clergy in various diſtant parts, letters were received; whoſe names, if known, would do honour to the Author. But, ſince the ſcheme proved abortive, it would not be right to make them public, any otherwiſe than they themſelves may have done it.

The failure was owing, partly to an un-lucky circumſtance known only to the Author; and partly to the worldly wiſdom of ſome, to-gether with the want of it in him.

A Meeting of a few reſpectable Clergy in or near London, was propoſed to be held, to draw up the Form of an Addreſs to the Biſhops; which the Propoſer had declared that he would not dictate. An intimation from the late Dr Dodd, that he wiſhed to be of that number, occaſioned the meeting to be brought on ſooner than was intended. in order to avoid a man, with whom the Author never choſe to have any connection whatſo-ever; and who, he thought, would do no credit to the meeting. It was held in Ten-niſon's Library. Dr. Yorke, then Dean of Lincoln, ſince Biſhop of Ely, was in the

C   Chair.

Chair. Dr Porteus, fince Bp. of London;
Dr. Percy, afterwards Bp. of Dromore, Dr.
Salter, Mafter of the Charterhoufe; Dr.
Owen, Chaplain to Bp. Barrington, and a
few more, were prefent. The Author, not
prefuming to take the lead; but, after having invited the Clergy, meaning to be led
by them, did not bring forward any Form of
Addrefs to the Bench In that he has perhaps
to blame himfelf for its mifcarriage. Had
he produced one, he faw little reafon to doubt
of its being figned (very probably with fome
little alteration) by the members prefent; who,
profefſing the greateft regard for the prefent
Church Eftablifhment, declared their wifh to
be, to have a revifal of the Articles and Liturgy, and the Forms of Subfcription (the very
fame as the Author himfelf had declared):
and who hoped to fet forward an application to the Bench of Bifhops, for that pur-
pofe. Had fuch a Form been then figned,
he had authority from feveral others in different parts of the kingdom, to fet their Names
to it.

In another particular the Author feems to
have

have been to blame. Being afked by the members prefent, what the bench of Bifhops thought upon the fubject; and whether he fuppofed they would approve of fuch an application? he did not think it became him to difclofe, what had paffed in private converfation with them; and waved giving any decided anfwer. In confequence of that it was, that the members determined, that the Drs Yorke and Porteus, fhould wait on the Abp. of Canterbury; and communicate to him their wifhes and intentions; and confult his Grace on the propriety of the meafure.

They did fo, on a day appointed by the Archbifhop, a little before Chriftmas; who replied, " That he would lay their wifhes be-
" fore his brethren, as foon after the holi-
" days as there fhould be a fufficient number
" in town: and in the mean time, he de-
" fired, that the matter might await their
" determination." His Grace then afked,
" Whether many of the Clergy in different
" parts of the kingdom were apprifed of their
" requeft; and concurred with them in it ?"
And, upon receiving an anfwer in the affirma-

tive,

tive, he added, " That he took it for granted
" there were many of the fame opinion;
" and that this application would fuffice for
" the prefent "

When the iffue of the meeting in Tenni-
fon's Library was reported the next morning
to one of the Bench, he feemed much cha-
grined, and faid to the Author, " Then there
" is an end of the matter This deputation
" will defeat your fcheme. A perfon may
" like to have an application made to him,
" and may not object to its being in ftrong
" terms, but he cannot afk for it." " Though
" you was unwilling to fay that the Bifhops
" approve of your plan; you might have
" faid, that you had good reafon to think they
" do not difapprove."

His Lordfhip's words were but too true.
The Archbifhop intended, as it was intimated,
to get a meeting of the Bifhops at Lambeth;
to confult together upon the affair· But his
benign intentions were overruled, by thofe
few who fet their faces againft the plan He
was perfuaded to afk opinions fingly: and
finding fome few very ftrenuous opponents
(among

(among whom was one great Biſhop, who had had the pamphlet above a fortnight on his table; and when preſſed, was forced to acknowledge that he had never read'd it, though he had argued vehemently againſt it), while others were ſhy of venturing to ſpeak out freely for it; the matter went no farther. Without any meeting of the Biſhops at all, an intimation was ſent, that the propoſed application to them would not be acceptable; ſince " it was neither prudent nor ſafe to do any thing."

There the whole dropped to the ground; and never was reſumed. The Author wrote immediately to all thoſe, from whom he had received letters of requeſt that their names might be added to the addreſs, to inform them of its failure. and he then conſigned their letters to the flames, that nothing might appear againſt them through his means. After having thus publicly, and he thought reſpectfully, borne his teſtimony to the Propriety, and what he eſteemed the Neceſſity of a Reviſal of the Forms of Subſcription in the Church of England; he then ſet himſelf

down,

down, with a confcioufnefs of the integrity
of his heart; which, fcorning fubterfuge,
could thenceforward fit at eafe after fo full
and public an avowal of his fentiments.

The propofed application to the bench of
Bifhops, put-by the Clerical Petition to Parliament, which it had been the intention to
renew in that Seffion But, a Petition from
the Diffenting Minifters, to be releafed from
fubfcription to moft of the Articles of the
Church of England; which had been received by the Houfe of Commons, and paffed
as a Bill in 1772, and had afterwards been
thrown out by the Lords; every Bifhop in
the houfe voting againft it (mifled by one,
who had declared at a meeting at Lambeth,
that he hoped they would all oppofe it, and
whofe overbearing temper they were each of
them unwilling to provoke by any expref-
fions of a difference of fentiment; who yet
deferted them by abfenting himfelf on the
day when it was known to come on) was
renewed again in 1773; and again thrown
out by the Lords; one Bifhop alone giving
his voice for it. This kept up the fubject in
the

the minds of all ranks of men, and occafioned frequent difcuffions, in private converfations and in print, during that whole year.
Though nothing was done in a public way,
either for the relief of the Clergy or the Diffenters, during that interval; yet thofe difcuffions which took place, prepared the way
for fome degree of eafe to both, in which
the Author of the Addrefs to the Clergy had
fome fhare.

The Debates on the Clerical Petition laid
open the glaring impropriety of requiring
fubfcription from the Diffenters: which, the
more it was canvaffed, became the more
clearly manifeft to every one. The Author,
being at that time in the habit of converfing
upon the fubject with various ranks and
orders of men, foon found that the defenfe
made by the greateft advocates for retaining
the Clerical Subfcriptions, pleaded more and
more ftrongly for the exempting of the Diffenters from it: and that the Lords Manf-
field and Camden were then become publicly their advocates; while the greater part
of the bench of Bifhops, were now afhamed

of

of having been mifled by a falfe Brother
into oppofing them. Perceiving this, he
did for the Diffenters what he knew he
fhould wifh to have done for him, had he
been in their cafe; and gave intimation to
fome leaders in the Diffenters committee, that
if they renewed their application in moderate
terms, they might expect to fucceed Though
it was delayed through fome differences a-
mong themfelves, the iffue proved him to be
in the right

The fame converfations during the courfe
of that year, led him to the thought, that a
publication of the effect of thefe debates
upon men's minds, might be of effential fervice to the peace of tender confciences, whether any alteration in the mode of Subfcription were made by any act of the legiflature, or
not. This gave rife to a Pamphlet, publifhed
at firft under the title of *Confiderations on the
State of Subfcription to the Articles and Liturgy
of the Church of England towards the clofe of the
year 1773* a Copy of which was put into the
hand of every member of each Houfe of Parliament, on the opening of the Seffion 1774.
The

The title was foon altered to *The State of
Subfcription to, &c.* to diftinguifh it from one,
publifhed about the fame time at Cambridge,
entitled, *Confiderations on the Propriety of requiring Subfcription, &c.* by the then Bifhop
of Carlifle.

In this Pamphlet, which Mr W. publifhed
under the fignature of a Confiftent Proteftant;
after tracing the origin of fubfcription to
Articles of Faith in general, and our own in
particular; what attempts had been made at
various intervals to foften the Terms, or to
releafe people entirely from any fpecific declaration upon fome fpeculative points contained in them, and what had been urged
more fully of late, from various orders and
defcriptions of men, both within and without
the pale of our eftablifhed Church, he gives
a ftring of refinements on the different manner in which fubfcription is underftood by
different *Defenders* of it. Various indeed they
are and contradictory to each other. Yet
is there no one among them all, but what
the Author himfelf had heard, or feen in writing, from fome of the warmeft advocates for
the

the continuance of fubfcription in the then
Form· and indeed for the moft part, from
thofe who had oppofed his former fcheme.

The Conclufion to be drawn from it was,
and indeed it was the defign of the publication to make known, that, however unfeeling
fome ftiff Divines and high-church Laity had
fhewn themfelves, in oppofing all applications
for relief, *their own interpretations* of fubfcription had given it. Thofe who could not
confcientioufly fet their hands to what they
did not fully and literally acknowledge to be
true, wifhed and petitioned to be releafed
from fuch a burthen; or to have the terms
foftened Yet the Defenfe which thefe rigid
ones had fet up, was fo compleat a departure
from the original avowed intent of fubfcription, that it had ceafed through their inter-
pretation to be any declaration of a man's
opinion at all. Subfcription had indeed pro-
feffed to be, "for the avoiding of diverfity
" of opinions " but thefe over-warm advocates for it, had *declared*, that a *latitude* of in-
terpretation muft be allowed, and indeed,
they affirmed, had almoft from the firft been
allowed,

allowed, in the underſtanding of the Articles and the Subſcription to them The Biſhop is to ſee them ſubſcribed by each perſon, before he receives any ecclefiaſtical appointment at his Lordſhip's hands· He is to reconcile that to his conſcience as he may. But, by theſe interpretations, the difficulty was removed. By the authority of the *moſt Orthodox* it was declared; that the Biſhop himſelf did not look upon it, neither was it to be looked upon, as any avowal of a man's ſpecific opinion one way or another Shameful as this is, and diſgraceful to the Church; yet is this the ground upon which Subſcription to her Articles has ſtood ever ſince, and ſeems likely to continue. And ſo that Pamphlet ſtated it But ſurely the Blame and the Diſgrace muſt lie; not on thoſe, who peaceably endeavored to obtain an amendment, by a reſpectful application to the Biſhops themſelves to propoſe it in the way they ſhould judge moſt proper, but on thoſe, who ſo unfeelingly and ſo ungenerouſly oppoſed it, at a time when it might have been done with eaſe.

The

The Times, not long after this, became very different. And then perhaps a ftrong Remonftrance from a large Body, might have demanded attention. But the Author of the Addrefs to the Clergy, never chofe to *force*, what was refufed to be granted to him on peaceable terms. He was urged to the attempt by One, who told him thofe were the feafons for carrying a point: and, that if a man fcrupled to make ufe of fuch an advantage, he muft never hope to fucceed. Yet was that method of procedure, not fuited to the Author's difpofition. Neither was it, what the Perfon who preffed it then, would himfelf have liked when he was afterward High in Office.

This Pamphlet was immediately followed by another, entitled, *Queries relating to the Book of Common Prayer with propofed amendments*. the occafion of which was explained in the introduction. When the Author of the Addrefs to the Clergy, propofed a revifion of the Articles and Liturgy, fome affected to object, that no particulars were fpecified, that he ought to have pointed out fuch parts as

appeared

appeared to him objectionable, which might
then have been taken into confideration; but
that fuch a vague requeft, could tend to no
good. A ftale trick: the conftant refort of
mean fpirits, when they do not intend to pay
attention to what is defired. But, to preclude
all reafonable objection, the Author no fooner
felt himfelf quite clear from thofe who kindly
had connected themfelves with him in the
application to the Bifhops, than he committed
his thoughts to paper. ftating them in the
form of Queries, for feparate and almoft de-
tached confideration, as moft refpectful from
a private perfon to the public.

Among them, many things were propofed
as Queftions to be confidered, which do not
offend him in the leaft; but which he thought
might be fpared, or at leaft might be foftened,
for the fatisfaction of others One Idea he
ventured to fuggeft, which he believes was
new, and he fears gave difpleafure at the
time, the impropriety of reciting any Creed
at all in a place of public worfhip during the
time of divine fervice To that, many perfons have fince acceded, who did not at the
firft.

firſt. But he muſt confeſs, that he has continued of the ſame opinion: That, however proper a Creed may be on certain occaſions, to which he means not to object; he ſees no advantage, but manifeſt diſadvantage to the cauſe of true Chriſtianity, in making any one, however general be its terms, a part of Common Prayer: more eſpecially in having three Creeds, and one of them ſo very objectionable in ſome expreſſions, as that called the Athanaſian.

Theſe Queries were unnoticed, as it was expected they would, by thoſe in authority; though addreſſed to them, and preſented to them But the Author had the ſatisfaction of hearing them commended by many whoſe opinions he valued, even before he acknowledged them to have come from his pen: and he has had that ſatisfaction many times ſince, from perſons to whom he is a ſtranger

For ſome months indeed, he was unwilling to be known as the parent of either of theſe two publications, after he would otherwiſe have divulged it; left the connection he had with Dr. Yorke then Dean of Lincoln, ſhould

be

be any hindrance to his advancement to the
See of St. Davids, to which he was deſtined,
but which for a long time was delayed. When
appointed by him to preach the Conſecration
Sermon, he deſired to decline it ; and begged
of the Biſhop to reconſider the matter, and
to conſult his friends : becauſe, though he was
ſenſible of the honour done him, and heartily
thanked his Lordſhip, he wiſhed and adviſed
him to think of one not ſo marked as Mr. W.
He prepared a Diſcourſe, which he truſted
would have given no offenſe, though it muſt
be treading on tender ground : but, on the
whole, he was not diſpleaſed when he was
releaſed from it.

A little before that time, the then Biſhop
of Wincheſter ; who, from his former ſtation
as Preceptor, was in the habit of much converſation with His Majeſty ; told the Author,
that " Inquiry had been made concerning
" him, in conſequence of his Addreſs to the
" Clergy." And the Biſhop added, ſeemingly
from himſelf, that " he hoped on the diſap-
" pointment of his ſcheme for obtaining re-
" lief, he would not ſecede from the Church "
This

This he urged, with greater force than really
was neceffary in refpect of Mr. W. againft
fuch a meafure   To that, he received an ex-
plicit anfwer immediately. But, that there
might be no miftake in words fpoken, as foon
as Mr. W. returned home, he wrote a letter to
his Lordfhip; explaining fully and freely his
view in the publication of the Addrefs; to-
gether with his fentiments on Subfcription.
Therein he declared, " That while all par-
" ties underftood each other, he could acquit
" himfelf of deceit in evading the literal and
" moft obvious meaning of words. That,
" with regard to his Function; he had fairly
" and bonâ fide entered into the Miniftry, and
" folemnly pledged himfelf to do his beft in
" it   and till it fhould appear clearly, that he
" ought no longer to continue in it, he
" thought himfelf bound not to quit it."
The letter was intended to be fhewn to his
Majefty, if the Bifhop faw proper. And it
is apprehended that it was   Its contents
certainly were communicated: the Bifhop in-
forming the writer foon after, that he was
rectus in curiâ

From

From that time all hope of seeing any amendment in our Formularies has ceased: and with it all endeavors on the part of Mr. Wollaston, though repeatedly urged to it by the inconsiderate. Indeed, notwithstanding he cannot but continue firm to the Cause of Truth, and cannot but wish most earnestly, as he has ever done in his heart, that the very shadow or suspicion of dissimulation, might be removed from the Clergy; the *Times* have been such, that He not only has ceased to move for any alteration, but has discouraged and would strongly dissuade any attempts towards it. He trusts, *with most full and assured confidence*, that TRUE CHRISTIANITY will in the end prevail over all opposition. But he knows that man must wait, till the Almighty Ruler of us all, judges that men are properly disposed to receive it. When that shall be, is yet in the womb of time. Perhaps, not many generations distant: For he has lived to see *the* BEGINNINGS *of a* VERY GREAT CHANGE *working in the world*. A few years more, may calm the blaspheming and ferocious spirit of the first

D   movers,

movers; who are moſt clearly mere *inſtru-
ments*, in the hand of *the* GOD whom they
deny, for purging mankind of their errors, and
forwarding the wiſe deſigns of HIS providence.
Then will all parties be brought to a more
firm *acknowledgement* of THE TRUTH; and
ſucceeding generations will ſee *Good* ſpring up,
out of the preſent accumulation of *Evil* Pro-
phecies ſeem to point that way.

Yet though nothing was done by Mr.
W which ought to give offenſe to reaſonable
men, he did not eſcape ill-natured aſperſions.
The few ſtrictures on his Addreſs to the Clergy,
he ſuffered to die in ſilence the death they
deſerved. His venturing to propoſe an alteration in the terms of ſubſcription, was inter-
preted as if he diſbelieved all the *Articles*.
His propoſing to concede in ſome points to
the wiſhes of thoſe, who could not reconcile themſelves to every part of our *Liturgy*,
was repreſented as if he himſelf wanted to
expunge the Whole. He was told that " he
had gone too far " The Orthodox called him
Socinian, as they now affect to denominate
every one who dares to differ from them in
any

any one particular, whatever way it chance
to be. Thofe who allow themfelves to be
Socinian, (which they now affect to call Uni-
tarian, as if none were Unitarians but they)
began to reckon him as almoft one of their
own number. Pamphlets, and even Books,
were fent to him from the one, to bring him
back to the acknowledgement of the Athanafian Doctrine, from the other, to call him
off from it. He read'd them all. And he
read'd them all with care, and divefted as,
far as he could from prejudice, being determined, as he had always been, to follow
whitherfoever Truth fhould lead. But, while
he guarded himfelf againft an obftinate adhærence to an opinion he had formed, he
thought it neceffary to be equally on his
guard againft too hafty a change A Dig-
nitary, high in rank in the Church of York,
he underftands it was, fent him a book publifhed under his aufpices; by which it has
been faid, that Mr. W. was reclaimed from
Socinianifm. Had that been fo, Mr. W.
readily would have acknowledged it. But
the truth is, no one ever was farther from

the

the leading Characteriſtic of Socinianiſm, than
he has been in every part of his life. For,
though a large ſet, nine folio volumes, of the
Fratres Poloni, were given to him by one
of that perſuaſion, he muſt confeſs that he
never could think of wading through them.
He was always willing to hear and to con-
ſider what any one could ſay on either ſide
of any queſtion, and thereupon moſt inclined to look into ſuch Authors as were
of an opinion contrary to his own: but the
little that he has dipped into any of thoſe
volumes, while ſufficient to prove to him
the ſincerity of the writers, did not ſo far
make him hæſitate, as to think it neceſſary
to waſte his time in diving deeper. What
he has heard in converſation, or read'd in
the writings of Prieſtley, (whoſe parts and
learning he admires, but whoſe injudicious
vehemence he laments) and of Lindſey (whoſe
conſcientious conduct he reveres) he thought
ſufficient, to give him an inſight into the
main force of what can be urged on that ſide:
but far ſhort were they, of bringing him to
accede to that opinion, or in any degree to

lean

lean that way. He ever did think, the Atha-
nafians the Arians and the Socinians equally
fincere CHRISTIANS and ALL *equally to blame*,
for denying that appellation to each other.
From that Opinion he will not eafily be
driven. To adopt entirely the interpretations
of either, he does not fuppofe he ever fhall.
But, whatever his own fentiments have been
on thofe matters, or whatever they may be,
he has been moft fully perfuaded, that he
ought not to call himfelf a Chriftian, if he
denies to others that liberty of underftanding
and interpreting the holy fcriptures for themfelves, which he claims on his part. This
he has always publicly maintained, and always muft maintain He fincerely wifhes
that others would do fo too.

This led him into taking the part he did
in behalf of the Diffenters, *on a matter of
confcience*, in 1774. But when, fome years,
after, they applied for a repeal of the Corporation and Teft Acts, the Cafe feemed to him
widely different. Mr. W was afked by fome
of the Bifhops, as well as others, what he
thought on that head. He does not pre-

fume

fume to flatter himfelf, that his opinion could be confidered as of any importance to the public decifion, but fuppofes it might be afked, by way of collecting the fenfe of various orders of men, or perhaps with a thought that he might poffibly have had fome knowledge of the Diffenter's intentions.

To that, he conftantly and invariably replied; " That he confidered this, merely as " *a political queftion*, in which he himfelf " prefumed not to give an opinion. He was " clear, and had always declared, that, in " refpect of a man's religious fentiments, the " State had no bufinefs, nor indeed any right, " to interfere, unlefs he made that a plea " for difturbing the Community. So far as " he invaded the peace of others, he muft " be refponfible to the Civil Magiftrate, " and liable to be reftrained by him. But " in refpect of Civil Offices, Mr. W. pretended not to judge, whether thofe who " are not of the eftablifhed religion, ought " or ought not to be admitted into them. " He always wifhed the Teft itfelf were " different from what it is. And he really " had

" had his doubts; whether the reftraining
" of the Proteftant Diffenters from fuch Of-
" fices, were politic, according to the politics
" of thofe who wifh all to be of one perfua-
" fion, inafmuch as it ferved to keep up a
" diftinction between them and the Church-
" men, who would before that time have
" coalefced, if they had been left to them-
" felves.

For his part he muft confefs, he cannot
wifh thofe diftinctions entirely to ceafe.
Though a true and firm friend, to the eccle-
fiaftical as well as the civil Conftitution of this
kingdom; he is clearly of opinion, that, con-
fidering the frailties and imperfections of men,
fome differences among us in our religious
and political fentiments, are of effential fervice, in keeping religion and politics on a
right footing, by obliging all parties to be
on their guard. It is little enough that any
of us do attend to our duty with thefe watches
over us: ftill lefs fhould we be inclined to
do things properly, if all the checques of op-
pofition were removed,

As

As to the late applications for the repeal of
the Corporation and Test Acts, Mr. W. must
add, that he has considered them as trials of
political strength, rather than as arising from
any religious or conscientious motive whatsoever Among the Dissenters, as among all
ranks and descriptions of men, there are the
good and the bad, the peaceable and the dis-
satisfied and in every community, the turbulent are those who take the lead. It is far
from certain, that the peaceable among them
have really any desire that it should be granted nay, many of the other description would
be disappointed of their aim, if it were; because their wish is, to raise a clamour And
they all know the Dissenting Interest would
in a few years be annihilated if once those
distinctions were at an end   Yet in the present state of things, that which might, and
which perhaps ought to have been granted
unasked, or to have been ceded to a modest
request from the peaceable, he thinks certainly ought not to be given up, to the threats
and arrogant demands of the turbulent The
vehemence of one or two Leaders, has hurt
the

the Diffenting Intereſt much, in the opinion of many a by-ſtander Mr W who honours the integrity of the Body in general, has been ſorely vexed at the indiſcreet conduct of ſome.

In the ſpring of 1777 he was collated by Dr. Yorke then Biſhop of St. Davids, to the Precentorſhip in that Cathedral. Nothing paſſed by way of animadverſion upon that promotion, which ever came to his ears. But two years after that, when he was preſented to the United Pariſhes of St. Vedaſt Forſter and St. Michael le Quern London, by the Dean and Chapter of St. Paul's, at the nomi-nation of Dr. Greene then Biſhop of Lincoln, he was not ſo happy. The diſappointed Curate of that Church, who had been recom-mended to the Chapter for that Rectory, to-gether with certain of the Minor Canons of the Cathedral, diſappointed on their parts too; were generally ſuppoſed to be the perſons concerned in miſrepreſenting his actions, not only in private, but in the public papers *.

Be

* Scorning duplicity at all times, and at all times hurt at the thought of a Clergyman, at his firſt entrance upon a Cure, being

Be that fuppofition true or falfe : They neither of them received one word of animad-
version

to interrupt Divine Service by Forms of Law, though he had
fo publicly exonerated his confcience from any fhadow of fubterfuge in his fubfcriptions and declarations, he thought it
became *him* to explain to the congregation, the reafon for what
he was then to read before them, and the authority by which
that was required   This he did in the following words

" Brethren   It feems neceffary that I fhould now interrupt
' your devotion, while I comply with certain Forms which
" are appointed to be gone through during the time of divine
fervice foon after our firft entrance upon a Parochial Charge,
" which, though Forms of Law, and foreign to Devotion,
' muft not be omitted while the laws of our country are fup-
" pofed to require our compliance

" The firft is a very old Form, of above 200 years ftanding ·
" whereby it is underftood that the Articles faid to be agreed
" upon in Convocation in the year 1562, commonly called the
" 39 Articles, are to be read'd in your prefence   and for
" which accordingly I muft in the firft place beg your Pa-
" tience '

After reading them, He then added

" Thefe are all the 39 Articles faid to be agreed upon in
" Convocation in the year 1562   of which it was ordered, by
" an Act of the year 1571, that fuch only as concern the Con-
" feffion of the true Faith, and the Doctrine of the Sacra-
" ments, fhould be read'd in the Church whereof we have the
" Cure, in the time of Common Prayer there   But as it has
' never been fpecified, by any Act whatfoever, which of the
" 39 Articles were intended by that defcription, it has been
" cuftomary

verſion from *him*. The latter were repri-
manded by the Members of the Chapter, for
the

" cuſtomary to read them all This I have therefore done
" accordingly, of which you have been witneſſes And now,
" in obedience to that Law, I declare my unfeigned aſſent
" thereunto.

" The next Law is one of a Century later, commonly called
" the Act of Uniformity of K. Cha II 1661 which requires,
" that after reading the Morning and Evening Prayers ap-
" pointed to be read'd by and according to the Book of Com-
" mon Prayer, of my having done which you now have been
" witneſſes, I declare my unfeigned aſſent and conſent to the
" Uſe of all things therein contained and preſcribed And that
" I make that Declaration in theſe words following which I do
" accordingly make uſe of for that purpoſe and no other. I
" Francis Wollaſton do hereby declare my unfeigned aſſent
" and conſent to all and every thing contained and preſcribed
" in and by the Book entitled the Book of Common Prayer
" &c.

" Of my doing this alſo, you now are witneſſes.

" But the ſame Law enjoins likewiſe, in a following clauſe
" which is a little altered by a ſubſequent Statute, that not-
" withſtanding this Declaration I have now made in a pre-
" ſcribed Form of Words, I ſhould read before you a Decla-
" ration made before the Vicar General of the Lord Archbiſhop
" of Canterbury, to much the ſame effect, though in a different
" Form of Words, of which this Paper is a certificate "

The Declaration, and the Certificate thereof, were then
read'd. after which He added,

" This

the illiberality of their conduct. The former
could receive no rebuke, excepting from his

own

This being done, the same Law is generally understood
' to require, that I should declare the same again in Your
" presence And therefore, I do declare that I will conform to
' the Liturgy of the Church of England as it is now by law
' established Which surely, every Minister of the established
" Church must be ready to conform unto, and ready to de-
" clare the same upon every occasion, though the repeating
' of Declaration upon Declaration he must esteem unneces-
' sary and the interrupting of Divine Service for these pur-
" poses, what nothing but the positive commands of certain
' Laws, made while the minds of men were warm with civil
' disturbances, yet still in force, can justify "

" However, of my compliance You now are witnesses And
' therefore, having gone through those Forms of Law, let us
" return to, what is more becoming this place, and my station
' among you, and resume our Devotions to Almighty God,
' asking His pardon for this interruption, and offering up to
" Him the concluding Prayer for this day's service "

This was represented, in a very illiberal letter in one of the
newspapers (manifestly shewing itself to be drawn up by a
person connected with some of the Minor Canons of St Pauls)
as if he had said that, " the business he was then engaged in,
' was both ridiculous and unnecessary, and that he begged
' pardon of his hearers for being guilty of it And that nothing
' but the prescription of the Church could impel him to it."
Had he run through the Ceremony in the usual way, the same
person would most undoubtedly have accused him of in-
sincerity.

own confcience, when he was convicted of fowing the feeds of diffention between the new Rector and his Parifhioners, by a mis-ftatement at the time when he meaned to relinquifh the Curacy; pretending it as a grievance that he was to be difmiffed; when in reality it was made clear to the leading Members of the Parifh, that he had underhand engaged himfelf to another more lucrative Cure (which he certainly had a right to do moft openly) after he was affured, not only in words but in writing, that he might have continued at St. Vedafts.

That he quitted it, was very foon found to be greatly to the fatisfaction of Mr. W.: becaufe it made an opening for Mr Prince to be recommended to him by one of the Churchwardens, than whom he could not have had an Affiftant more compleatly to his mind, and he believes to that of the Parifhioners in ge-

---

It is very poffible that fome may think he was indifcreet, in adding any words from himfelf yet it appeared to him to be but proper, in his cafe. He might judge wrong for he is not exempt from error But it certainly did not deferve the rancour with which he has been purfued, in confequence of fuch an indifcretion; if an indifcretion it was.

neral,

neral, and whom he was forry to lofe, when, after ten years diligent attention to the Parifhes, he could not but bear due teftimony to his merit, on his being propofed for the Chaplaincy of the Magdalen Hofpital; to which he has indeed proved himfelf a Treafure.

It fo happened that the late Curate's coming to Chiflehurft, finally to fettle the affair of the Curacy, whether he chofe to continue it or not, firft gave-rife to a Matter which has occafioned much talk, and which has not been without its confequences. On mention being made concerning the *Society for promoting Chriftian Knowledge*, to whofe late fecretary the curate was allied by marriage; he offered, and thereupon was authorized, to propofe Mr. W. as a member. He did fo. But, though he feldom failed in his attendance at their meetings, he was abfent on Tuefday Sept. 7, 1779, the particular day when the Election came on. He was informed of the event directly. But it was not till four days after, he wrote a letter, expreffing " great concern at being to " notify to Mr W. his having been rejected " by every Member prefent; who feemed

4   " afhamed

" afhamed of what they had done, by having
" ordered that no entry fhould be made of
" it on their minutes, but whofe names he
" would tranfmit to him, if defired, at a
" future opportunity."

Mr. W. by the return of the poft, defired,
" that none of the names might be fent to
" him; left he fhould be led thereby into
" entertaining an unfavourable idea of any
" particular perfons; which he fhould not
" if they were unknown. He lamented
" that a Society profeffing to be Chriftian,
" and for the promoting of Chriftianity, fhould
" reject a perfon willing to contribute his Mite
" to their good defigns, for no reafon he could
" conceive, but becaufe he had expreffed a
" wifh to fee Chriftian Charity exercifed to-
" wards thofe who differ from us: But he
" begged, that if he deferved fuch a ftigma
" from the Society, they would not fcruple to
" enter it fairly on their minutes." He did
not mean the letter for them, but for his
curate. However, in order to prove that He
was in Chriftian Charity with the Society, he
inclofed a draught for £. 20; which he defired

fired might be prefented to their Treafurer at their next meeting, as a teftimony of his good will towards them.

In what colours Mr. W. had been reprefented to them, fo as to occafion his rejection, he knew not. But he trufted that this conduct in him, could give no offenfe to the Society at large, however it might touch the confciences of fome. He meaned *them* no harm: He wifhed their refipifcence. To his aftonifhment, the money itfelf was rejected by the Board And what would have been accepted by them with thanks, and probably with exultation from the moft reprobate libertine, it was not thought fit to receive from him.

Thefe are the naked Facts.

The return he made to this behaviour, was to let the whole remain in filence And at laft it was through fome of them, that it ever came forth, and he was obliged to explain the Matter Till *his name* appeared in the public papers, he difregarded all allufions to the affair, and never once mentioned it himfelf to any one. When it was made public, he difdained to inquire after the Authors of the

paragraphs;

paragraphs; or to make any reply whatfoever, or any remarks upon them; but only fhewed to fuch of the Bifhops, and moft refpectable members of the fociety, as well as others who afked him concerning it, the very letters which had paffed on the occafion.

Here it might be imagined that malice had vented its fpleen. But it was found to be otherwife. In a converfation two years after, with Abp. Cornwallis, concerning the *Society for the Propagation of the Gofpel,* his Grace offered to propofe Mr W as a member. To that he replied, " that he would very chear- " fully contribute to the purpofes of that fo- " ciety; and fhould be proud of his Grace's " recommendation. but he thought it in- " cumbent on him, previoufly to let his Grace " know what had paffed at the other Society; " and, if he wifhed it, to fhew him the letters." Mr. W. was however propofed. But before the day of ballot, the Secretary of that Corpora- tion called upon him by the Archbifhop's order; to let him know, " that an anonymous letter " had been received at Lambeth, faying, that " Mr. W. would be rejected: and therefore

E　　　　　　　　" his

" his Grace defired to know, whether he
" wifhed his name to be withdrawn." He
waited on the Archbifhop the next morning,
and told him, " That he fhould be much vexed
" that any one honored with his Grace's
" countenance, fhould be refufed admiffion as
" a member · otherwife, that he was himfelf
" indifferent about it. He was very certain
" that he had never done any thing to deferve
" fuch treatment from any perfon whatfo-
' ever; and therefore had confidered his re-
" jection at the other fociety, as reflecting
" greater difgrace upon them, than upon him-
" felf." The Archbifhop faid, " He thought fo
" too · but it had appeared to him proper to
" apprife Mr. W. of the letter he had re-
" ceived, though, fo far as related to him-
" felf, he fhould not regard it, and he cer-
" tainly would not withdraw the name un-
" lefs Mr W defired it " The name was not
withdrawn The Archbifhop propofed it in regular courfe, at the third monthly meeting of
the Board The ballot was taken One negative was found on opening the box. But,
as it is always the cuftom on fuch an event, to

repeat

repeat the ballot; left one fingle negative, which would decide the election, fhould have been put in by miftake, on taking it a fecond time, the votes were all in the affirmative. Mr. W was admitted at a fubfequent Meeting.

Upon thefe facts each perfon will put fuch a conftruction as he judges right · Mr. W. thought himfelf juftified in afcribing the anonymous letter, to thofe who had been moft active in the flight paffed upon him by the Society for promoting Chriftian Knowledge. Indeed that feemed to be fully confirmed feven years after; by a fimilar mifreprefentation of his reading-in at St Vedaft's, revived, and officioufly communicated from them to his Grace's fucceffor, inftead of feizing an opportunity, which with Mr. W's confent was afforded them by the Bifhop of Ely, of retrieving the character of a Chriftian Society, by fhewing Chriftian forgivenefs towards a Brother, whom indeed they once, nine years before, had *fuppofed* to be in fault; but who yet had never done any one thing fince that time to which the moft cenforious could ob-

ject;

ject; and whose only offense towards them had ever been, the offering to open his purse, perhaps a little wider than was customary, to forward the professed design of their institution. That was the sole reason, ever alleged by any of the Society to him, for the rejection. An Error, if that allegation had been the truth, very easily to be rectified.

However, by their pertinacious adhærence in 1788 to a decision in 1779, of which they themselves had been ashamed, and by their endeavors to injure his character with our present Metropolitan, as they had in vain attempted with the last; they have placed him on the higher ground. Yet shall not that move him to shew the least spark of resentment towards a *respectable* Society. As a true Disciple of Jesus Christ, he must still hold himself ready, to give them the right hand of fellowship, if ever they shall think fit on their own motion to reconsider the matter, or intimate any inclination to have it moved, and to hold forth theirs. As to those Individuals who could suffer themselves to behave so illiberally, they are beneath the notice

of

of Mr W. in any other way; than by declaring, as he now does thus publicly, that whoever the Leaders were in 1779, or in 1781, or in 1788, (whose names to this day he knows not, and wishes not to know) they have forgiveness from him. May they return to a better mind: and may they be forgiven of the Lord, who knows the truth of every word that is here related, and the secrets of all our hearts.

Yet has not all this been without its consequences. Finding his labours in the ministry of the Gospel, so liable to be misrepresented; through the unchristian perverseness of some, who yet profess to be teachers of it, he became disheartened· his spirit has sunk on the thought of ascending a pulpit; his zeal has slackened; he has felt a disinclination to attending any large assemblies of the Clergy; and at length it has determined him, to prosecute his endeavours in the line of the Profession no farther. For him to write on any subject in Divinity, could now do no service. There would be an obstinate renitence in those, who affect to appropriate orthodoxy to

E 3 themselves

themselves, against receiving any thing from his pen · though in respect of the greater part of the articles of our Church, he is no farther distant from the literal orthodoxy of it, than they are But to enter the field of controversy never was his ambition · He always lamented the acrimony with which it is usually carried on And he clearly saw, that He could not attempt to render himself useful beyond the boundaries of his own Parishes, and scarcely within thofe in London, without expofing himself to much obloquy.

Thereupon he turned his mind to a pursuit, which had afforded him much comfort in thofe times when the Doubts concerning Subfcription engaged his anxious thoughts the ftudy of Aftronomy. To that he has dedicated much more time than ever had been intended by him, or than ever would have been bestowed by him upon it, had he found he could employ thofe hours in the walk of his Profeffion, with any profpect of advantage to Markind In Aftronomy he trufted, that he fhould be at a diftance from any of the jealousies, any misreprefentations of narrow-

minded

minded bigots. That is a walk, far above their comprehenſion. There he could allow his thoughts to range, without fear of giving offenſe. He could look up to the heavens, and adore his Maker, and admire His works, without preſuming to pry into His Eſſence, or daring, or even entertaining the moſt diſtant wiſh, to conſign to eternal perdition, thoſe who do not ſee things juſt in the ſame light, or judge of them juſt in the ſame way, as himſelf

By Aſtronomy he was led in thought, far beyond this ſublunary world of ours, and all its petty ſquabbles, and to ſuppoſe, that thoſe vaſt bodies he diſcerns above, muſt be peopled with their ſeveral gradations of inhabitants, and thoſe inhabitants muſt be objects of the Divine favour, as much as man. And ſince it is not improbable, that ſome among ſo many may have been found diſobedient, he muſt ſuppoſe that, if they ſtood in need of Redemption, they have been redeemed, or may yet be to be redeemed, in ſuch way as the Almighty judges beſt ſuited to each. To confine his thoughts to this earth of ours, never was the Syſtem of his *Religion.*

To

To contend, Whether the Eternal Deity himself took human nature upon Him, and became a " perfect man," according to the Athanafian Syftem; or whether a " mere " man," i e a perfect man, was infpired, or guided, or fuperinduced by an afflatus from the Deity, according to the Socinian Hypothefis; always appeared to him much more nearly allied in reality, than either of the parties would choose to grant. A Difpute it is, perhaps at the bottom, very little more than a difpute upon words. while the Doctrines built upon this foundation, on either fide, by fubtil diftinctions, and forced conftructions, and the acrimony of Cenfure *in both parties* towards each other, on a Matter not fathomable by the human underftanding, he moft certainly muft ever hold to be *unwarrantable* and *unchriftian*.

But the Idea, that THE ONE ETERNAL, SELF-EXISTENT DEITY, furrounded by myriads of Angels and heavenly Spirits, may have *created* man by the miniftration of THE ARCHANGEL [THE *Archangel Michael*, the λόγος, or *Word* of God to us] and may have

configned

confized the fuperintendence of man upon
this earth to *him*; and by *him* revealed His will
to the Ifraelites; and by *him*, *redeemed* mankind;
fending *him* in the Form of man, yet as His Son,
the SON OF GOD, into this World of ours; to
be the Mediator, the only Mediator between
God and men; not to reconcile God to man
(the holy fcriptures talk not that language)
but to reconcile man to God, to inftruct
man in the will and the ways of God; to be
an example to mankind, to die for man; to
rife again, by the power *committed* to *him*;
to afcend into heaven; to intercede for man;
to receive the prayers, and conduct the af-
fairs of *his* Church, till *he* returns again in
glory to reign in *his* kingdom, and judge
mankind, before the confummation of all
things, when *he* will deliver up the kingdom
to GOD, even the Father,—this Idea (Cavil-
lers fhall now be told) has feemed to the
Author, moft confonant with thofe holy Scrip-
tures, which he folemnly *and confcientioufly*
promifed, when he entered into holy Orders,
to make the *fole* Rule of *his* Faith. And that
the HOLY SPIRIT OF GOD, fhould be commif-

4 fioned

fioned by the Deity, to guide and inftruct mankind; has appeared to him agreeable to the voice of Scripture, and to have nothing difficult in the conception · though the whole of thefe things he does not pretend to under-ftand, and there are many queftions may be afked which he prefumes not to refolve Ne ther has it feemed to him to be any forced conftruction of language, to call the com-munications by either of thefe Spirits, com-munications by or from God Neither is it unreafonable or unfcriptural to allow, that other Spirits may at times have been fent on various occafions to Man

This leaves the Mind open to the thought, that communications in the fame way, by the fame or by others of the Angelic Hoft, may have been made to the rational inhabitants of other Sphæres And furely fuch a thought, if not within the limits of what has been efteemed Orthodoxy, cannot merit very fevere reprehenfion

To quarrel with any one about it, HE never did, NOR EVER WILL That would cer-tainly be deferving of cenfure, becaufe it is

contrary

contrary to Chriſtian benevolence, that *Teſt* of a *truly orthodox* Diſciple of Jeſus Chriſt: more eſpecially ſince theſe are Matters which cannot as yet clearly be known; and on which he is as liable to miſtake as another man. Neither would HE ever perplex an audience with ſuch enquiries Enthuſiaſm may miſlead a perſon, into greater warmth in defenſe of an opinion which he *ſincerely* holds, than is proper; or than in his cooler moments he may judge right, but the true Chriſtian ſhould beware of being ſo miſled An *unuſual* opinion may be broached by ſome, and maintained by ſophiſtry, with a view to diſplay their parts or their learning · Or an *eſtabliſhed* one may be profeſſed by others, and ſupported with dogmatic pride, and ſharp cenſure on thoſe who queſtion its truth; in order to bring a man into notice, and pave the way for Preferment Theſe things are not uncommon. But whoever is guided by *the true Chriſtian Spirit,* will abhor all ſuch practices.

To Aſtronomy therefore, Mr. W. gave up much of his time: thinking therein he could render himſelf uſeful to mankind, without

inter-

interference from *those* brethren of the cloth; who never have *thought enough*, to know what it is to *doubt*, or to have any feeling for those who do and whose ungenerous conduct towards him, so unlike that of Gentlemen or of Christians, has sometimes tempted him, in the frailty of human nature, to repent of ever having condescended to enter into the same orde with *such* Men

As to the higher preferments in the Church, his friends have at times thought he looked towards them , and some did suppose he certainly would have been called to them . more especially when he was surrounded by Ministers of State, and had two of the Cabinet among his Parishioners, with whom he had lived in habits of intimacy For his own part, he never was ambitious of the parade attending an exalted station. He knew his own comfort and that no situation in life could be more to his satisfaction than that in which he had the happiness of being placed, and in which it had been his study to make himself respected and beloved. Could a larger sphære enable him to do more good, he would not

shrink

ſhrink from it: but he queſtioned whether it could be deſireable enough, for him to ſollicit it. Perhaps it might enable him better to provide for a family of ſix Sons and nine Daughters, who have lived to grow up But it certainly would tend to enlarge his expenſes, and their ideas: and very poſſibly he might not find himſelf able, ſo well to come up to them On their account therefore, as well as his own comfort, had it been ever ſo certainly in his power to force himſelf into preferment, he always doubted much whether it would be adviſeable to him. His connections indeed made it not quite impoſſible he might have ſucceeded, had he been ſollicitous for ·advancement and his being told once, that he muſt not be diſappointed if the next Biſhoprick was not conferred on him, becauſe it was intended for another, ſhewed that ſome perſons thought ſuch a thing not unlikely. Yet many may think that probabilities were always againſt him, and many, that he never was equal to ſuch a ſtation. Be that as it may. An Iriſh Biſhoprick was at one time indirectly propoſed to him by way of exchange:

change and he believes that arrangement might have taken place, had he approved of it but he never hæsitated one moment on that head One of the smallest of the English ones, he some years ago did intimate a wish that he could obtain above all others, because that was such as would not have called him away from Chislehurst, which he had always determined he never would leave while he could retain it · but a little coldness in the reception, put by the thought entirely, which never was resumed His name once got into the papers for the Bishoprick of St. Davids; and so far gained credit, that he was asked by expectants concerning the preferment he should quit: but a name is often read'd in a newspaper, without its ever having been in the contemplation of the Minister

His *Ambition* has been, to render himself as useful in the World, as those circumstances and that moderate share of abilities which have fallen to his lot, have enabled him to attempt: and his *endeavours* have been, to educate a very large family in those sentiments In respect of himself, he has had the happiness of

being

being provided *entirely to his comfort*. In refpect of his Family, they have for the moft part *fulfilled his wifhes* There is no fituation in this world without its rubs, but he ought to acknowledge, and be thankful, that he has had lefs than his proportion of them Too far advanced in life to expect he fhall be capable of doing much more, in any Station, his hope and his aim of late years have been, to get the feveral branches of his family rewarded, for that deep fenfe of religion, that ftedfaft loyalty, and that indefatigable attention to their refpective occupations, which he feels the fatisfaction of having inftilled into them with fuccefs; whereby they *may deferve* the notice of the Public, and, whether noticed or not, they certainly *will fecure* the BLESSING OF GOD, and their own Comfort.

22

Publications by the same Author,

Sold by G. *and* T. WILKIE, N° 57, *Pater-Noster-Row.*

———

An ADDRESS to the Clergy of the Church of England in particular, and to all Christians in general Humbly proposing an Application to the Right Reverend the Bishops, or through their Means to the Legislature, for such Relief in the Matter of Subscription, as in their Judgements they shall see proper together with the Author's Sentiments of the present Forms, and his Reasons for such an Application. 6d

The State of SUBSCRIPTION to the Articles and Liturgy of the Church of England, towards the Close of the Year 1773, with a View of its Progress from the Beginning, and of the Alterations that have been made in it by the late Debates Recommended to the most serious Attention of the Three Estates of the Realm 1s 6d

QUERIES relating to the Book of COMMON PRAYER, &c with proposed Amendments Addressed to those in Authority, and submitted to their Consideration 1s

A DISCOURSE on the NATURE and USE of CONFIRMATION 6d

The Preface to a Specimen of a general ASTRONOMICAL CATALOGUE, arranged in Zones of North Polar Distance and adapted to Jan 1, 1790, giving an Account of the Work which is now in the Press, and what may be expected in it 1s 6d

A GENERAL ASTRONOMICAL CATALOGUE, arranged in ZONES of North Polar Distance, and adapted to Jan 1, 1790 containing a comparative View of the mean Positions of Stars, Nebulæ, and Clusters of Stars, as they come out upon Calculation from the Tables of several principal Observers, together with a Proposal for setting on Foot some regular Method of observing the Heavens, through the concurrent Assistance of Astronomers in all Nations, in order to form a more perfect Register of their present State, and discover any Alterations to which they may regularly be subject, or which they may at any Time hereafter undergo. 3l 3s in boards.

Two

Two SERMONS preached in the Parish Church of Chisle-hurst in Kent The First on Friday, April 19, 1793, being the Day appointed for a General Fast The Second on Sunday, June 2 upon reading his Majesty's Letter in Behalf of a Collection for the French Clergy 1s

A SERMON preached in the Church of the united Parishes of St Vedast Foster, and S Michael-le-Quern, London, on Friday, February 28, 1794, being the Day appointed for a general Fast 1s

Directions for making an universal MERIDIAN DIAL, capable of being set to any Latitude, which shall give the Mean Solar Time of Noon, by Inspection, without any Calculation whatsoever 1s

ALSO

A CŒLESTIAL PLANISPHÆRE, for assisting Students in Astronomy in learning the Principal Constellations Engraved and sold by John Cary, No 181, sold also by William Cary, Optician, No 182, Strand

Preparing for the Press.

A CATALOGUE of STARS within 25° of the North Pole, observed by the Author with a Transit Circle (described by him in the Phil Transf Vol LXXXIII p 133) and reduced to Jan 1, 1800 Together with a Map of that Portion of the Heavens on a large Scale

☞ It is apprehended that it may yet be two years before the result of these Observations can be thought worthy of the public eye But an Astronomer who shall wish to have any particulars communicated to him, shall freely have what information can be given him, upon application to the Author,

22

CPSIA information can be obtained
at www.ICGtesting.com
Printed in the USA
BVHW022328290123
657409BV00006B/135

9 781140 704225